Just About Anything

NEW AND SELECTED POEMS

Books by Jonathan Aaron

Second Sight
Corridor
Journey to the Lost City
Just About Anything

Just About Anything

NEW AND SELECTED POEMS

Jonathan Aaron

Carnegie Mellon University Press
Pittsburgh 2025

Acknowledgments

Grateful acknowledgment is given to the following magazines in whose pages these poems first appeared:

Narrative Magazine: "Lightning Time"
The New Yorker: "Acting Like a Tree," "Listening to Richter"
Raritan: "Big Numbers," "Just About Anything," "'Oaty'"
The Times Literary Supplement: "Prepositions"

"Cedar Waxwings" appeared in *Bright Wings: An Illustrated Anthology of Poems About Birds*, edited by Billy Collins.

"Elsewhere," "Kurt Schwitters' Real Name," "The Wolf of Gubbio," "Skills," "Disappearances," "Tisane," "Van Gogh and the Wind," "The House," and "Destination" are from *Journey to the Lost City*, copyright 2006 by Jonathan Aaron. Reprinted with the permission of The Permissions Company, LLC on behalf of Copper Canyon Press, coppercanyonpress.org. All rights reserved.

"The Heart," "From the 1929 Edition of the Encyclopedia Britannica," "Sufficiency," "The Children's Crusade," "Recalling the Huns," and "The Sighting" first appeared in *Corridor*, copyright 1992, from Wesleyan University Press.

"The Hydrant," "Here Everything Is Still Floating," "Giacometti's Dog," "Guests," "Memories of the Dictator," and "The Spell" first appeared in *Second Sight*, published by Harper & Row in 1982.

Book design by Connie Amoroso

Library of Congress Control Number 2024942063
ISBN 978-0-88748-713-2

10 9 8 7 6 5 4 3 2 1

Rebecca, always

It still isn't noon; it's tomorrow morning.

—James Schuyler

Sometimes my life opened its eyes in the dark.

—Tomas Tranströmer

Contents

New Poems

Selected Earlier Poems

New Poems

1

Human Behavior

I used to be a moody loner
who gave street corner sermons about angels
dancing on the heads of pins.
But I could never figure out exactly
how the soul is supposed to change into a bird.
One Fourth of July the Mayor got up
and recited "Barbara Frietchie."
I hadn't heard it since high school.
"You sure know your John Greenleaf Whittier,"
I said. He lunged at me. A scuffle ensued.
Apparently I hit him with a brick.
Then I settled down with the right woman
and started a family, putting food on the table
as a researcher in the dark sciences
at a large Midwestern university. Although
the ancient Greeks were right about practically
everything, the classical tradition never resulted in
a better world. After all, in Plato's Athens
people were routinely stung to death by bees.
The phone rang. My wife was calling to report
a sizeable insect crawling around in the bathtub.
I hurried home, opened a window, and shook
the fluttery wedge of next-to-nothing out
of a coffee cup into the afternoon, pondering
how history moves in mysterious ways.
It shows human behavior, for example, emerging
over a long period of time, like the Himalayas.
Later on, my dog and I were walking
in the neighborhood graveyard, dark-green
clouds above and beyond the headstones, when
a man in rags staggered from behind a tomb.
"I never used to be this way," he announced,
opening his arms like a welcoming host,
"but in the old country we always saw bats
in the evening—magnificent bats."

The moon appeared, and I remembered, too.
I could smell the springtime softness of the earth.
I could see the soul turning into a bird.

Dreamland

It's dark, so I step carefully.
The slightest false move could topple those
books stacked next to
the bulky shadow of an armchair.
Or that column as tall as I am
of how many others
leaning against the window trying to see
what the world is coming to
three stories below. Or those shelves
bearing the weight of no doubt
hundreds of tomes
no one has paid attention to since before the war.
I'm in a quandary, scratching my head,
wondering which way to turn, what happens next,
when a breath of air out of nowhere
touches my face, and a voice
softly inquires, Wouldn't you rather be home in bed,
lying back on a couple of pillows,
the little lamp beside you shedding just
the right amount of light as you turn
another page of one of those paperback thrillers
you so often count on to get yourself to dreamland?

Not of This Earth on the SYFY Channel

Waiting for my friend to pick up the phone,
I noticed the trees were shaking
the silvery undersides of their leaves
as if they didn't know what to do
with their hands. He's not home, I thought.
"Hello?" "It's me." "I can't talk now.
I'm watching *Not of This Earth* on the SYFY Channel."
Dusk was starting to confess its habitual
indecision—to rain, or not to rain,
to flow past quietly, or instead produce
a dozen sky-high robots wrecking the countryside.
I sat there trying to recall that sinister
hematologist from another planet,
his black suit and hat, his crucial sunglasses.
Then I remembered the old story
of a man who was struck by lightning
and on waking up in the hospital
discovered he'd become clairvoyant.
There's a planet out there no one's thought of yet,
he declared. And pointing at a nervous intern,
You are going to win a Nobel Prize.
He didn't know he was speaking
in Aramaic. No one else did either.
What's it like coming back to life and discovering
you're fluent in a dead language?
What's it like realizing the dark night
of the past is turning into a thing of the future?
I saw a doctor writing something on a clipboard,
a nurse shrugging her shoulders, pink roses
in a plastic imitation-crystal vase.
I could hear the telephone ringing
—my friend calling back.
"Terrible acting, totally unconvincing x-ray eyes!
Ludicrous production values! And yet,
and yet—a masterpiece!"

He was beside himself.
I was at a loss for words.
Nothing serious is easy to talk about.

When It Became Clear Aliens Were Working Here,

in memory of Stephen Dunn

Stephen, not surprisingly, declared it "the moment
mankind has been waiting for—the chance
to shake hands with the Universe," knowing, as he does

by heart, the best lines from the original version of
The Day the Earth Stood Still, which always reminds me
that the dynasty ruling China from the early

seventh century to the early tenth, part of the period
reflected in the dictionary of grave sites at a Xinjiang
location called Astana, was in fact the T'ang,

and that the works of over 2,000 poets from that time,
though often ghostly in their pale, nearly invisible
English disguises, continue to remind us how extraterrestrials,

perhaps from the very beginning, helped mankind
appreciate the ups and downs of everyday life.

Among the Russians

A bunch of us were sitting around a table
next to one of those big ceramic stoves
lazy good-for-nothings like to stretch out on
during cold winter nights. Nikolai Gogol
was holding by what he called its "ears"
an iron cooking pot. "I have ruined the vegetables,"
he said, meaning the stew of potatoes
and leeks we had all been waiting for.
Now we had no idea where dinner
could come from: the larder was bare
except for a few wizened turnips.
Anna Akhmatova gazed at him with something
like sympathy. Isaac Babel kept on reading a book.
Leaning back in his chair, Maxim Gorky
smiled at the ceiling. Poor Nikolai, who,
feeling "guilty and cursed," had burned part two
of his masterpiece, *Dead Souls*, just before he died,
was staring out the window. I looked
over his shoulder and saw what he saw—
darkness arriving with its flock of devils and witches.

Rendezvous

in memory of Charles Simic

I'm sitting at my usual corner table
savoring a bowl of chili when she walks in.

The look on her face as she hurries toward me
tells me I'm about to find out

what's on her mind. Leaning close,
she whispers, *"Foxfire, Elf Fire, Ignis Fatuus—"*

You must have mistaken me for somebody else,
I ought to say, but I'm too involved in this spicy

conflation of tomatoes, kidney beans, green
peppers, jalapeños, onion and garlic and morsels

of beef, all infused with turmeric, coriander,
and a slight suspicion of bitter chocolate.

She waves her hand as if warding off a mosquito
or the evil eye, whereupon the dim bulb

in my head brightens into something like
a memory: *The phosphorescent glow that leads*

people astray over swampy ground at night.
"Hold on," I say. "Try this—it's really good."

She hesitates, then accepts my spoon.
Her eyes widen. "No," she declares,

"It's fantastic!," takes some more,
and asks in another tone of voice,

"How come you never told me about this place?"
I can't explain.

It's as if we've known each other all our lives.

Overheard

—Wait a second. Don't move. There's a big spider sitting on your shoulder.

—I'm not surprised. A full moon always signifies the Weird.

—Just to be clear about this, I don't always mean what I say.

—I know exactly what you mean, but spider or no spider, the bay looks lovely, and tonight
      Pliny the Elder is coming to dinner.

—Remember all those wasps eternally buzzing around the grave of Archilochus?

—No, but I can't forget that summer day in the Forum when snow started falling on all
        those premeditating lions.

Heat Wave

A famous English movie actor is recalling John Wayne
on a transatlantic liner reading *Hamlet*.
I turn off the radio and open a window.
The fire escape shakes with each step of my zigzag
descent to a sidewalk so hot
it takes me a moment to notice the woman
in a plain white dress standing beside me.
She's cradling a bouquet of red roses
and looking beautiful as a glass of water.
I recognize her instantly—
I've been dreaming about her for years—
feel light-headed, weak at the knees.
A limousine pulls up. As soon as we get in, I notice
the glint of a bottle half-hidden in an ice bucket.
This is more like it, I'm thinking, and the touch of her hand
tells me she thinks so, too. Now we're passing
the Cathedral of St. John the Divine. I tell her
it's a lot cooler in Denmark this time of year, then add
more champagne to her glass, and more to mine.
Our flight is scheduled for late this afternoon.
There's really no rush.
Everything we need is where we're going.

Who's Thinking About the Last Time It Rained?

Not the painter in his studio
trying to throw himself into
his fugitive vision of a mountain lake.

Not the new bride carefully closing behind her
the door of a "honeymoon suite"
as the taxi she called idles on the street
three floors below.

Not the pianist performing in the recital hall,
his head full of Beethoven, his hands
a cloud billowing above the keyboard.

Not the Valkyrie in shining leather
maneuvering her black Harley
through the immobilized traffic on MacDougal Street.

While, far from the city,
in the silence of an empty house,
the Dog Star's breath still hot on the back of your neck
you can hear the first shy tap-
tapping of what you've been waiting for.

Big Numbers

Sometimes, after I start getting nervous about
how far it is to the nearest galaxy or back to
the late Cretaceous, or imagine the universe mindlessly

streaming away toward some final cosmic nothing
at all, I remember Mr. Wizard on TV saying,
Don't forget, kids, big numbers have minds of their own.

But I wasn't prepared for what happened early this morning
when, the rain over, shreds of ground mist vanishing like baby ghosts,
a full-grown Gazillion stepped from behind my neighbor's barn,

trailing way more zeros than I could possibly count
in the long moment it stood there looking around,
baring its teeth and flexing its brilliant feathers.

Arnold

A boxer-bloodhound mix, brown and white,
four, maybe five years old, he appeared out of nowhere
and sat down beside me with an inquiring look.
Such intelligence in your regard, I thought,

stroking his forehead, such wise forbearance
in your demeanor, scratching behind his ears,
Arnold, I said to him, good dog, I said,
how is it I already know your name?

He leaned against my knee. Nothing told me
I was about to wake up, not in Chicago
but in Bangor, the air cold, the night silent
save for the occasional whisper of a passing car.

Beethoven

Hearing the final moments
of his Symphony No. 1, I know
that only the Hillary Step
stands between me and the summit
of our planet's highest mountain.
But I'm low on oxygen,
I can't feel my toes, the wind
is shifting, so I turn off the radio,
lie down on the sofa, and close my eyes.
Now I'm standing at a lectern
in the a planetarium, but instead of
giving a talk on Jupiter's moons,
I'm reading aloud from a book
of poems by someone whose metaphors
scare the hell out of me.
The audience starts hooting and whistling—
after all, they didn't pay good money
just to listen to a bunch of wisecracks
about the end of the world.
Hold on, I say to them. This is important.
A bell rings. I wake up. It's already dark.
I reach for the light switch, then
think better of it. In the window,
snow on the trees turns into moonlight.
At fifty-six, Beethoven wrote
on the score of his last string quartet:
"Must it be? It must be."
Wind thumps and fumbles around the house.
On the other side of the world
great mountains are still
inhabited by gods.

Lightning Time

after Jacques Roubaud

To say it's wrong to say the lightning is pink
is nothing other than to say it's not the case
the lightning is pink, it's to say
the lightning isn't pink, and this isn't
something you could say
of the proposition "the lightning is pink," but
a somewhat more complicated sentence
about the lightning.

By the same token, to say
X thinks that the lightning is pink
means nothing other than
"X thinks the lightning
is pink," or "the lightning is pink,
thinks X," which is not
the same as, and, moreover,
doesn't even begin to resemble
the proposition "the lightning is pink,"
but is, or is like, a somewhat
more complicated phrase
about the lightning,
and about X.

And yet it was summer, it was evening,
and the lightning was blue.

The Mongols

What makes me think of them now?
Do I really need to remember
their sudden eruption out of
Asia in the early 1300s?
Their legendary archer-horsemen?
Their uncanny tactical mobility?
Their ruthlessness?

That in 1221 they reduced the great city
of Merv, "The Mother of the World,"
the Jewel of the Silk Road, its population
of half a million,
to a vast stretch of polluted ruins?
That when they left Baghdad seven years later,
it, too, had practically ceased to exist?
That, with a little more patience
they could have cut through Hungary
and Poland and reached the Atlantic?
That if they had, the world
wouldn't be the world
we still manage to think it is?

That their empire, greater than Alexander's,
fell apart after a paltry fifty years,
when Chinghis's sons and grandsons
started quarreling about the future?
That their unwritten law code spelled death
for entire peoples, yet allowed
freedom of religion and required
kindness to beggars and the elderly?
That they treated horses and certain dogs
with ceremonious respect?

That even today in rural Mongolia,
parents to whom misfortune

has been predicted sometimes give
their newborns names such as
Not This, No Name, Don't Know,
Nobody—"avoidance names"
with the power to confuse evil or jealous spirits,
cloaking their targets, spoiling their aim?
Since after all, who and what a person truly is
has always been anybody's guess.

2

Lateness

in memory of John Hurd Willett

When we were kids in Western Massachusetts,
you liked saying that Corsican shepherds
were your mother's people, and sometimes
you'd recite one of their hard-bitten adages:
Si rispetta il cane per il padrone—
Respect for the dog, respect for the master.

But here we are in your dilapidated
Land Rover, slowing down on a bridge
over the Ardèche, rattling on
about Albanian blood feuds, Romania's
legalization of witchcraft, contradictory
prebiblical concepts of the afterlife.

I mention a recent *New York Times*
report full of statistics showing
the average life span of the American male
to be seventy-seven years and nine months.
Tell me about it, you say, downshifting
as the road narrows.
Your genial Doberman yawns in the back seat.

*

In a small color snapshot,
you're sitting in front of that bar
on rue de l'Abbaye,
about to finish
a pint of beer, your expression wry,
intent, exasperated.

*

I step off the train, look around,
walk through a tunnel to the parking lot—
you're not there, either.
I find a table outside a café facing the station.
A few pigeons waddle near the doorway.
Hearing the train leave,
I tell myself that from time to time
it's all right to vanish for a while.

Two policemen approach.
The older one studies my passport,
taps his palm with it.
I'm waiting, I explain, for someone
who seems to be running late.

When they've gone, I order a coffee,
a second, then a third along with
a shot of Calvados.
I hold the little glass of amber liquid
up to the light, take a sip,
and pour the rest of it onto the pavement,
saying your name.

Alma Mater

I'd sit in the back of the classroom,
my head full of expletives
aimed at whoever
looked like they might be learning
something.

Dorm life was a fiction
for all except the survivor
of his high school motorcycle gang,
who liked rushing the corridors
on a Royal Enfield he kept
I never found out where.

The institution's "whiz kids"
dropped knives
down stairwells and were sometimes
suicidal, while the girls mostly
managed to keep
their wits about them.

Weekends everyone
congregated in off-campus
apartments, or lay down together
for warmth, etcetera,
in darkened student lounges,
one in particular
overseen by an art nouveau mural
featuring Progress
dressed in a transparent nightgown.

T. S. Eliot murmured on a podium,
a perfect bullseye in the spotlight's glare.
Billy Graham walked
the aisles of another year,
microphone in hand, explaining

Sartre and Kierkegaard
and God.

A distinguished German professor
of medieval history fell silent
halfway through his lecture
on the Albigensians,
placed on the desk in front of him
a finger-sized blue and white
plastic statuette
set in what looked like
a tiny bird's nest,
and struck a match—

the future showing us
something else it had in mind.

Just About Anything

When I got home, three policemen
were standing in the hallway muttering
into their cellphones, shaking their heads.
You'll hear from us, one of them told me
as they left, but we think you'd be smart
not to stay here for the next few days.
I called my boss and reported a family emergency,
then my wife, who was visiting her mother,
and booked a room at the nearby Marriott, hoping
I'd have a chance to get back to
Pride and Prejudice, or at least *The War of the Worlds*.
A few days later I received a call.
Our investigation is still in its early stages,
the voice explained. What we understand so far
has to do with how you define Reality,
which our forensics people say is like a ball
of yarn some universal cat is always playing with,
a concept maybe hard to get your head around,
though these days, in fact, one teleology
is as good as another. That evening,
old friends begged to differ. Solving your problem
calls for an appeal to the infernal gods:
you dig a pit, fill it with flammable materials,
toss in a few handfuls of rosemary and mugwort,
and light a match. It doesn't always work,
but you owe it to yourself to give it a try.
Thanks, I said, I will, thinking I would.
But sometimes I find myself of too many minds
when it comes to, you name it, just about anything.

Herpetology

Though I began to suspect
my landlady wasn't home,
I kept knocking—but softly,
since I was a new tenant
and wanted to be polite.
Who is it? she called.
It's me. I'm sorry to bother you,
but I've just found a very large
snake in my room.
She opened the door.
A snake, you said?
Moments later we opened
the door of my little studio.
Ah, yes, she said, nodding
toward the reptile in question.
That's my husband.
She touched my arm.
I know this sounds strange,
but every so often
the mood comes over him,
and he turns into a python.
In a day or two he'll be back
to himself again, right
as rain. Mind you,
he'd never hurt a fly
when he's in this condition
—though if he were less of
a humanist, I suppose . . .
She went no further, turning instead
to address what we were gazing at.
George, she said gently, George,
it's time to go home.
George lifted his large triangular head,
and after giving us
a brief once-over began

unwinding from the purple sofa,
feet upon feet
of him now soundlessly
flowing past us
onto the landing and down
the stairs. And with a quick
backward glance at me,
a finger to her lips
—and with was it a smile?—
she too was gone.

"Oaty"

One day, driving east from Chicago,
I noticed a little pony, brown with white socks,
standing alone at the edge of the highway.
I pulled over and got out of the car,
and when he turned and looked at me
I recognized him. "You're Oaty!" I exclaimed,
"my special pony!" He trotted up to me,
nodding emphatically, then knelt on his forelegs,
rolled over, and waved his hooves in the air.
As I rubbed his stomach I thought of
my family's abandoned farm, its ramshackle
barn, its fields of unmown hay. "Oaty,"
I said, "good pony, I'm taking you home."
He got to his feet and reared up, towering above me,
blocking half the sky. He wasn't a pony at all,
I realized, but a draft horse—maybe a Clydesdale
—mythic, tall as a monument.
From a nearby house I phoned the police,
who arrived soon afterward in a moving van
used only, one officer confided, to transport
the very largest animals friendly to man.
Tonight, years later, as I turn off the light,
Oaty is standing out there among the apple trees.
He comes and goes as he pleases, by mysterious means.
I try not to worry about his vanishings
or guess at their purposes. "Oaty," I say each time
we meet, "Oaty, wise horse, mighty horse."
And he lowers his head to mine, as if to confirm
with his intelligent, regretful gaze
that he knows much more than I do. Which he does.

To a Fruit Fly

Tiny one, teetering red-eyed on the rim
of my empty wine glass, don't fly away—
I'll pour another for the both of us.

Acting Like a Tree

When I got to the party and saw everybody
walking around in Christmas costumes,
I remembered I was supposed to be wearing one, too.
Bending slightly, I held out my hands
and waved them a little, wiggling my fingers.
I narrowed my eyes and pursed my lips, making
a *tree face*, and started slowly hopping on one foot,
then on the other, the way I imagine trees do
in the forest when they're not being watched.
Maybe people would take me for a hemlock,
or a tamarack. A little girl disguised as an elf
looked at me skeptically. Oh come on!
her expression said. You call that acting like a tree?
Behind her I could see a guy in a reindeer suit
sitting down at the piano. As he hit the opening
chords of "Joy to the World" I closed my eyes
and tried again. This time I could feel the wind
struggling to lift my boughs, which were heavy
with snow. I was clinging to a mountain crag
and could see over the tops of other trees a few late
afternoon clouds and the thin red ribbon of a river.
I smelled more snow in the air. A gust or two whispered
around my neck and face, but by now
all I could hear was the meditative creaking
of this neighbor or that—and a moment later, farther off,
the faint but eager call of a wolf.

Russian Studies

The other night I was lying in bed, my nose in a book,
when my dog jumped up beside me.
"What's that you're reading?" she asked.
"A history of Russia in the 20th century," I replied.
"You mean Lenin and Stalin, the Great Purge,
the show trials, World War II, etcetera?"
"You know about this stuff?" I asked.
She poked my shoulder with a forepaw.
I noticed her nails needed trimming. "The book—
what does it have to say about dogs?"
"It's a meditation on human nature,
so it's got nothing to do with dogs." "Look,"
she said, "don't you agree that, historically speaking,
no animal is more basic to human experience
than the dog?" "I do." "And isn't that why
you told your granddaughter there's no sound
in the world quite like a dog's barking
on a rainy night?" "Of course." "Then obviously
what you're reading about has to have dogs in it."
I thought for a moment. "Well, I can't recall
any dogs in Solzhenitsyn." She stared at me.
"Read him again," she said. "More carefully."

Prepositions

in memory of David Ferry

They're supposed to help us talk about here and there—
In your pocket, on the street, under the table.

About then and now—It's finished between us.
Come back to me. What will I do without you?

About when and where—The day before yesterday.
Down by the riverside. Over my head.

But what they really mean is: *This* way? *That* way?
As if I'm still lost one night years ago

in the suburbs of a strange city, asking directions
of shadows who've no reason at all to speak my language.

The Fantods

*". . . there laid a man on the ground. It most give me
the fantods."*
—*Huck Finn*

This place gives me the willies, said Gabriela,
jiggling her leg. The heebie-jeebies,
said Stephen as he poured himself another scotch.
Look, said Larry, my hands are shaking.
Police sirens howled outside, and I remembered the fantods.
When I was a kid they were always loitering
on street corners, dressed in filthy blazers, shorts,
and beanie caps, shirttails out, ties askew, their grins revealing
many pointed teeth. One day they chased me
into an alley and took my lunch money, then
started poking me with sharp sticks.
Hey, one of them said, you could put somebody's eye out
doing that! and they started laughing so hard
they failed to notice I was getting away.
Today, I thought, they'd be about my age, so-called
adults, with jobs and even families of their own.
But then again, maybe they're still out there
in the dark, waiting for me. Rain rattled
at the window like a fistful of pebbles,
and I came to my senses. We were still discussing
clairvoyance, spontaneous combustion,
the legendary feathered serpents of ancient Peru.

Here We Go Again

The narrow hallway
leads me to a half-open door.
I step past it, not sure
I should, and find myself
in an ill-lit room,
face-to-face with
an elderly woman
leaning on a cane.
Signs of the zodiac
glimmer on her dark shawl.
Taken aback, I ask
Can I help you?
I ought to ask *you*
that question, she says,
but my vision is limited,
cataracts, you know.
I'm due for an operation.
One of these days
I'll see like an angel.
She looks around, squinting.
Now that you're here,
she says, I see no point
in waiting. It's
late afternoon, time
for an aperitif.
Why don't we go
to that nice little café
just down the street.
I'll be your guest.
She reaches for
a beat-up valise tied shut
with a length of twine.
My spirits lift.
The lindens are blossoming,

the birds are singing,
and I'm almost positive
it's not going to rain.

Visiting the Master

Standing at his desk
next to an open window,
portly, wearing a peruke,
he was writing
in a hefty ledger
with a feather pen.
"Herr Bach?"
He turned and glared.
"Forgive my barging in,"
I said, "but I've come
from the 21st century
to inform you
that in the era I live in
you're not just a legend,
you're a god
whose creations are crucial
to sustaining the human spirit
in an ever more
troubled world." I paused,
wondering whether to mention
the discovery of electricity,
Edison's genius, the latest in
audio technology,
the atonal music
of the spheres.
But Johann Sebastian
(I didn't actually call him that)
was already steaming.
All at once a bird in a tree
just beyond the window
started singing.
As both of us stood there,
surprised and charmed
by its uncomplicated song,
from elsewhere in the house

came the sound of breaking glass,
then of voices raised
in laughter or argument,
I couldn't tell which.

Cedar Waxwings

A dozen of them dodged and fluttered
in the branches of the thirsty rhododendron
being drenched by our backyard sprinkler. Some perched
among the leaves holding their wings open to the water
as others, a little apart, shrugged themselves dry.

I lost count as more kept arriving
in their black burglar masks, brown or black
throat scarves, olive green jackets and crested hats,
yellow trim at the end of their tails. Those in command
flaunted bright red flashing near their wingtips.

What, I wondered, could have led people in past times
to regard these birds as harbingers of death?
They're tame and sociable. They call to each other in flight.
Several may sit together on a branch
or wire, passing a piece of fruit back and forth,

beak to beak, sharing the taste. Mating pairs do this
with flower petals. An adult can hold
as many as thirty chokecherries in its crop
and regurgitate them one by one into the mouths of its young.
They love to party. Sometimes they get so drunk

on overripe berries they keel over
and then have to sleep it off.
The branches they flocked on bobbed and sagged, the air
was full of their gleeful gibberish.
Not one of them weighed more than an ounce.

A Couple of Crows

Side by side on a low branch, bobbing their heads
and uttering muffled guffaws, no doubt making fun of
what's going on here—pinheaded jays speeding by,
robins poking in the grass for worms, dithering
squirrels, three or four rabbits unready for anything,
and slack-jawed me staring up, thinking
that if I understood their language
I might be laughing my head off, too.

A Few Things I Learned from Aldo Buzzi

in memory of Mark Strand

That both Russia and the United States are "ignorant of the bidet."

That "According to Hesiod, [crows] live nine times longer than man, and ravens even longer."

That one of Chekhov's terms of endearment for his wife Olga was "little cockroach," and that in his "medicine chest" he "kept a revolver."

That Vladimir Mayakovsky said to Sergei Yesenin, "Better in fact / to die of vodka / Than of boredom."

That ". . . Tolstoy preferred Harriet Beecher Stowe . . ." to Shakespeare.

That "[E]ven in antiquity literary prizes tended to be awarded to mediocre works."

That ". . . the great physicist Ettore Majorana . . . let his hair grow very long, like a generous portion of *scuma* (foam), the finest spaghetti, thinner than angel hair, . . . in order not to waste precious time at the barber's. As the young Stendhal did, too."

That "[when] Proust was asked who he would like to be if he had not been Proust he replied, 'Pliny the Younger.' But he was only fourteen."

That basil ". . . as the peasants teach, must be watered at night."

That "yesterday I did nothing."

That "I see my mind has wandered."

That according to Heraclitus, "The living and the dead, the waked and the sleeper, are the same."

The Subjunctive

is the verb form
we use to express
the contingent or
hypothetical
nature of an action
or event
presupposed to be
"contrary to fact."
It subjoins
conditions generally
not in keeping
with how
we perceive
the "real," as when
the facts surprise us
and leave us
mystified, at sea.

Take, say,
that photo
everyone knows
of a bullet tearing through
a haughty-faced
king of spades.
Or the blurry one
Rimbaud took
of himself
in Abyssinia,
looking as if
he's just been rescued
from aliens.
Or that voice
on the History
Channel telling you,
"It was here

that the Spartan
Shangri-la
would reveal
its darker side."

It's a strangely
luminous warehouse
at the edge of town.
It's the not
knowing how to say
I love you
in Arabic.
It's got nothing
to do with
the Soviets in Estonia
in 1941
listing who
they plan
to get rid of,
starting with statesmen,
soldiers, and lawyers,
and ending with
tuba players
and stamp collectors.

No,
the subjunctive
signals the fanciful,
or a special kind
of dreaming—
John Clare, for instance,
once called
"the peasant poet,"
now recognized
as a master

conjurer of weather
and wildlife,
wishing,
in one of his
elevated moods,
he were a fly.

Bearing in Mind

My wife and I in a crosswalk arguing
about bad movies, the sudden bus
barely missing us, our reflections
wavering in a plate glass window
while we catch our breath.

On a footbridge in Venice, moths
in a streetlamp's glow, my friend pointing
at the stone-carved name of a narrow
waterway we weren't looking for:
Calle dei Morti.

The visitor from another language
drawing a tiny flower
in my copy of his *Selected Poems*,
spelling "cordially" with a single "l,"
then smudging his signature.

3

Big Ideas

As someone who has trouble thinking
about big ideas, I'll occasionally
pick up a book of philosophy
in hopes of sharpening my so-called wits.
I don't go in for helpful "commentaries"
designed to show the way for
readers like me. I only want to find
that single sentence lying at the heart
of the matter, the kernel
of kernels, the source of the light I lack.

But now, just as I start suspecting
I can see X's concept of phenomenology
actually taking shape in the words I've been
staring at, its charm, its subtle glow,
I notice it's raining, and the laundry
hung on the clothesline, and more
hammering down in the cellar, where
a team of experts is looking for what
they tell me I'm a lot better off
not knowing anything about.

Orthography

I often write the word "cheese" with the letter *z*.
When I do, somebody I can't see mutters, "Not again."

I know "cheese" is spelled with an *s*—I've always known
it's spelled with an *s*—but since the *s* in "cheese" sounds like a *z*,

each time I hear myself say "cheese," *z* declares itself, the way it does
in "breeze" or "freeze" or "sneeze," or even "knees."

In a dream I keep having I'm desperately trying to spell "cheese,"
at my wits end and wondering if I'll ever learn. I stare

at *s* and say, "Hello, quick wiggle in the rainless grass,"
then at *z*—"Hey, little zigzag flickering out of a dark cloud."

The Treaty of Versailles

. . . what was past, still is.

The famous history professor had just delivered his lecture
on the Treaty of Versailles, especially Articles
227 and 231, i.e., the one demanding
the Kaiser be extradited from the Netherlands
for trial back in Germany, the other
imposing billions in war reparations.
I was exiting the auditorium, still thinking about
June 1919 and all those world-class diplomats
who couldn't even see eye to eye on the weather,
when a woman caught up with me and said,
I thought refreshments were going to be provided.
It was the beautiful dental hygienist
who had cleaned my teeth not three weeks earlier.
She liked to hum as she worked,
and tended to say "Rinse" with a little laugh. Well,
I said, I came here to find out more about
the Treaty of Versailles, especially Articles
227 and 231. My wife disapproves. She calls it
a bad habit, so it's a weight I carry.
She stared at me. Really? My boyfriend thinks
I'm crazy because I'm always wondering why
the past won't stop repeating itself.
You'd think it had better things to do with its time.
Exactly, I said. For me, it's the Treaty
of Versailles. That's just what I mean, she replied.
Who knows what yesterday, in its infinite
wisdom, is going to pull on us next?

Reality TV over the Atlantic

Still on edge an hour after takeoff,
I manage at last to get the tiny screen in front of me
to light up. The headphones don't work,
but I start channel surfing anyway, and settle on
a guy who's hanging from a helicopter
high above what must be a rainforest.
He grins, crosses himself, and tumbles
toward the twisting emerald ribbon of a river.
Now he's running beneath vine-clustered jungle
canopies shining in what must be a monsoon rain.
Wait a second—he's underneath a capsized trimaran,
wide-eyed, looking around. Or rather, he's trying
to haul himself up, or stuff himself into,
a narrow passage leading toward, or away
from, a flooded cave. I'm getting confused.
He's sitting in a tree in maybe the Serengeti.
He's got a rope. What's he doing with it?
Tying a knot and staring up at something
I can't see. It's dark. Oh no, he's in another cave
holding a torch. He reaches into a jagged cranny
and extracts from it a black spider with extremely long legs
that's struggling frantically on the point of his knife.
He winks at the camera and licks his lips.
He's walking unsteadily in a sunbaked landscape.
His eyes are slits, his forehead bulging hydrocephalically.
Maybe he just encountered a swarm of bees.
Maybe it's something he ate.
A passing flight attendant leans toward me
with a question. Rather than ask her to repeat herself
I smile and say, *No thank you,* since I believe
it's important to be polite to anyone
who's doing the best they can to help the world
not crash and burn.

Little Elegy

in memory of Joseph Brodsky

After a night in the shaky
but mysteriously comfortable guest room
bed, he materializes in the kitchen,
still only half awake.

"How'd you sleep?" *"Terrific."*
He sits at the table. Sips a cup
of black coffee, gets up, goes outside
for a smoke or two.

Returns a few minutes later, heads for
the fridge, opens it, stoops into its cold glow.
"I see ham. I see a chicken leg.

Do you have any meatballs?"
And with a grin adds,
"Times like this, nobody dies."

Inside a Goose

So I'm thinking of the ancient Romans, who,
on special holidays or anniversaries or
the death of an emperor, would roast a chicken

inside a duck inside a goose inside a pig
inside a cow, a feast that might help account for
why civilization is never more than seven meals away

from anarchy, and reminds me of how often I
experience without understanding
things I'll never be able to get my head around.

If Only He Knew

Doors slam and shades flap. An open book
next to the window gets speed-read by the Invisible Man.

Birds fly backwards upside down.
The little wooden farmer on the garage roof saws faster and faster.

Wind chimes are a monkey on the xylophone.
A ray of sunshine shakes across the golf course, showing

Benjamin Franklin lofting his kite and key,
while someone just behind him looks terribly pleased with himself.

Omens

Loud banging on the back door
turned out to be my next-door neighbor George.
His house was spectacularly on fire.
Come on in, George, I said, and gave him a hug.
You and Emily can stay right here with us.
Emily isn't answering her phone, George said.
She's supposed to be visiting her mother, but
I think she may have run off with Fred.
He collapsed in a chair next to the kitchen table,
his head in his hands. She wants to buy a new car.
We've been arguing about it for weeks. Fred, and now
this, he said, gesturing at the conflagration.
A wild look twisted his face. I must be cursed.
Hours later, the firemen gone and George's house
a blackened ruin, we found ourselves taking a break
on my front porch. He reached for my offering of
another brew. Where do I go from here? he asked.
I'm too old to reinvent myself.
George, I said, I've got a butterflied free-range chicken
in the fridge, marinating since yesterday
in olive oil, lemon juice, garlic and rosemary.
There's enough for the three of us, and for Emily, too,
in case she turns up. I'll just throw it on the Weber.
Maybe how the smoke behaves will give us a sign.
The sky darkened, a few crows rose noisily out of a nearby oak,
lightning flickered. Then George's cellphone rang.
It's Emily, he said, wide-eyed—*Hello? Hello?*

Baltic Rain

I set *Faceless Killers* down
on the bedside table
and turn off the light,
my thoughts still following
the delusions of yet another
homicidal weirdo from the brain
of Henning Mankell, Sweden's
master of the detective thriller.
Maybe tonight I'll dream about
Stockholm, where, aged ten,
I was considered too young
to see a movie I'd already seen
back in America—
The Furies, a B-western in which
Barbara Stanwyck throws
a pair of scissors at Judith Anderson,
aiming for her eyes. The Swedes are
famous for their welfare system,
their sturdy cars, their alleged
open-mindedness about sex, but they admit
that during their sun-famished
winters a special kind of moodiness
can make even a naturally cheerful
person feel cut off at the knees.
I can see Kurt Wallander,
Mankell's detective, sitting alone
in his apartment drinking
aquavit and wondering
what it's like to believe in God.
At this point, it's probably raining
all over Skåne thanks to
a storm front stretching east across
the Baltic as far as Lithuania,
where hardly anyone recalls
the shtetls my father's forebears

came from, those far-off figures
slowly making their way
through heavy forests and clouds
of ancient superstition.
Given what finally happened, I wonder
whether I'd have had the wits,
let alone the means, to get out in time.
If people only knew
what lies in store for them,
thinks one of Mankell's characters
just before he steps into a phone booth
and finds out for himself.

Listening to Richter

I'm cooking pasta and listening
to Richter playing Brahms's Second Piano Concerto.
You're watching television in the other room.
"It's Johnny Depp," you call out. "Did he make a vampire movie?"
Richter's piano teacher likened him to an eagle.
He flies at great heights, he said, *and can see the landscape*
of music in all its vastness. Yet he has an unerring eye
for each and every detail. "Oh!" you call again. "There's
Gregory Peck! He looks like Abraham Lincoln.
How come he's in a boat?"

(Wits, etc.)

Last night I finally decided to take a crack at
a novel by Carlo Emilio Gadda (i.e., *That Awful Mess
on the Via Merulana*), reputed by a friend to be
a masterpiece. After reading the first few pages
I got out of bed and wrote down on the back
of an envelope a few words from I didn't know where
that I could still hear echoing in my inner ear
—this and that, a jumble, what have you, but maybe, I thought,
bits of a message, pieces of some half-cancelled memory
trying to animate the remains of my sense of things.
Was I gathering my scattered inner belongings
(wits, etc.) the better to listen? But listen for what?
I waited. And then it came to me. Your voice.

Knocking

after Jacques Prévert

Who's there?
Nobody
It's only my heart knocking
Loudly
Because of you

But outside
The little brass hand on the wooden door
Doesn't move
Doesn't stir
Not even the tip of its little finger

I Look Up

from the book I'm reading
and hear no footsteps, no doors opening or closing

no sounds of water being run in the bathtub,
no faint cough of a toilet flush. No one

in the kitchen laughing or speaking quietly on the phone,
or about to walk into the room and say thank you

to five aging sunflowers leaning from a vase.

Presence

I keep finding myself walking from room to room
as if I'm the ghost, you the one deep
in your favorite chair reading a magazine
or talking on the phone or about to tell yourself
it's time for lunch. Then some hint of my presence
occurs to you, and you raise your head
and get to your feet and glance around,
trying, trying against your better judgement—
you were ever skeptical—to understand
the nature of my stubborn lingering.

Ashes

They took only a few seconds to pour
from the shiny container into a hole in the ground,

but after all it wasn't you anymore, you were
past the borders of algebra and helium, past

where the universe comes to an end and then continues
as nothing—nothing

and everything.

Breath

The air cools suddenly.
Hey, I can see your breath—

No, you say, that's not my
breath. It's yours.

I open my eyes.
I grope for the light switch.

Night

Night rising out of the earth like smoke
as the ocean shuffles its cards
and rabbits play at the edge of the garden.
Night filling the valley, overtaking horses and cows
left in the fields, the single still-lit window of a house.
Night, hooded, its flowing depths of black linen
noiseless except for the sound of a door closing
somewhere down the road, a dog's bark,
a whip-poor-will's call from the moody
hollow, a little wind in a stand of scrub pine.
Night, the moon on its forehead like a miner's
lamp whose glow discovers the cemetery's
cherry blossoms and, on a headstone,
a pair of spectacles, forgotten or left in memory,
the number *8* tipped over on its side.

Looking at the Moon

Never the same as you proceed
through your calendar of moods,
some nights hurrying against the clouds,
on others motionless,
as if waiting
for music, or the sound of a footstep.

So far from what all of us have tried
and keep trying to make of you,
staring up at you asking
questions no one can answer
but asking anyway.

When rain or snow obscures you, or
when you occasionally disappear
behind your own shadow, is it only
habit of mind that keeps me from thinking
you've ceased to exist—the same habit
reminding me, once you reappear
in bone-white wonderment,
that the craters and canyons on the other side of your coin
are full of slow-moving
perspectives that will never include us?

The Museum

What could have possessed me to forget
how late it was?
The high-ceilinged corridor looked deserted,
but the hurried footsteps echoing everywhere
couldn't have been mine alone.

I heard the slams of electrical switches being thrown
as one after another the galleries
I'd been hanging around in all afternoon
fell dark.
At the bottom of a flight of marble stairs

an elderly guard was standing next to an open door.
As I walked past him, he spoke to me:
Otto Dix is a god.
Surprised, I was about to say,
I couldn't agree with you more,

but the door had already closed behind me,
and I found myself out on the sidewalk, the museum,
a shadow of its former self,
slowly disappearing like a ship in fog
for parts unknown.

The Years

There's no lunch or dinner or satisfaction in the world
equal to an endless walk through the streets of the poor,
where you must be wretched and strong, brothers to the dogs.
—Pier Paolo Pasolini

1
You're at a disadvantage, being young.
What you know is good for the moment,
but gradually disappears into the distance behind you,
or abruptly when you make a sudden turn
onto a street smoking with rain. It's the years
that give you what to talk about.
You have to wait. You have to bide your time.

2
There's a pit
I drop into,
or there's the sky,
toward which I
unaccountably
rise.

Heraclitus

In saying that no one steps into the same river twice,
Heraclitus might have been arguing against
a prevalent belief in demons.
Character is destiny, he said. And also:
being dead is worse than being dung.
He came from Ephesus.
He lived from 535 to 480 BCE.
His life is a mystery.

Of what he wrote, little more
than a hundred fragments come down to us.
When you pick up one
it can sting and make you shake your fingers,
or feel like you do when
you're talking to someone who can't understand
what you're saying because you yourself
have no idea what it is you're trying to say.

The Obvious

Red geraniums waving at a season passing in seconds—
a yellow leaf I pick up here and lay down there—

we either think with the blood, or the air
or the fire inside us. With "a lonesome glee," said

Emily Dickinson. I take my pulse,
wondering what's the good in the world

coming apart at the seams. How can you
put the pieces together when nothing's left

to begin with? From a standpoint of pure reason,
the obvious is incomprehensible, so it's hard to know

whether meaning anything has to do with meaning anymore.
Lao Tzu: "A good traveler has no interest in arriving."

Or the gentle refugee: "You can take your umbrella,
you can leave your umbrella."

Or Joseph Cornell: ". . . violet-banked approaches; musical waterfalls . . .
easy walking distance to enchanted lake

. . . reasonable rates."
Every memory has a mind of its own.

If it never happened, it's not as if it didn't.

Selected Earlier Poems

FROM *JOURNEY TO THE LOST CITY*

Elsewhere

for Stanisław Barańczak

It's almost noon. You put down your book
and look around. A cat stirs in its sleep
on the windowsill, fishermen are passing below on their noisy,

brightly colored boats, one of the two women at a nearby table
laughs, a peach glows
on the plate next to your glass,

and, in spite of the hour, the sound of a trumpet playing
"Stardust" waveringly
makes it all the way over from the other side of the harbor.

Kurt Schwitters's Real Name

He believed, with Heraclitus,
that the sun is only as big as it seems to be.
—Jean Arp (from his elegy for K. S.)

Kurt Hermann Eduard Karl Julius Schwitters:
"I am a painter, I nail my pictures together."
He loved nonsense, he said, because he felt sorry for it.
After the war, since everything had broken down,

the new could only be created from fragments.
Merz—a syllable that bears repeating until
it starts to mean what it says—rescued
by chance one day in 1919

from a newspaper advertisement
for the Kommerz-und Privatbank.
The word declaring itself for the first time
like one of the big electric signs flashing

above the seething streets of Hannover or Berlin.
What's left of commerce without community,
an echo of the Roman god of thieves,
four-sevenths of the German word for pain.

Merz, he decided, was his own real name,
and the name for everything he'd go on to make
from scraps of trash and refuse.
But his *Merzzeichnungen*, or Merz drawings,

his sketches with wastepaper, he couldn't help portraying
a vista. Take *Merz 19*, this little
stained glass window hinting
the ghost of whoever leans in

for a closer look at a war tax stamp
from a pack of cigarettes, potato ration stamps,
a streetcar ticket, the number 37,
remnants of Saturday

and Sunday, wrapping paper bearing the design
of an impossible labyrinth—everything
in the process of lifting like a flock of pigeons,
slowly, then more urgently,

into a glimpse of rushing cloud and sky.
Aphorisms for the eye
framed in snatches of an exploded grammar
(what other kind was there?)

about not enough food, a ruined currency, crowds
in lines, uncertain destinations,
the indifference of time. And the pale-blue
cutting of an unused registration form

like a premonition
that he himself would eventually become
to all but a few
someone who never existed.

In a photograph his son took in 1947,
he's alone on a distant knoll
in England's Lake District,
brightness and overcast,

water, then hills in the distance.
He always believed in landscape.
He never forgot the line of the horizon.
He hated throwing anything away.

The Wolf of Gubbio

It was one of those towns with practically no perspective,
the architecture half geometrical, houses upon houses
stacked at dizzy angles. Clouds the shape and color of laurel leaves
hung in a pale-blue sky. The locals walking around wore
guilty looks, conscious as always, of having something to hide.
Flowers grew in doorways, abundant, untended, extending
themselves in gestures of inquiry and yearning. Iridescent songbirds
plunged through the air, heedless of what might be waiting
in the forest at the foot of mountains that appeared
deliberately jagged. An angel, robed and golden-haired,
floated absent-mindedly above a garden. Farther off
and smaller in scale, a bat-winged devil, whose grimace
augured either laughter or tears, crouched on a rooftop.
A lake, or possibly the sea, gleamed at the distant end of a road
that wound through other towns, each a staid collection of arches
and towers like bunches of white asparagus in the noonday sun.
Saint Francis like to sing in French and knew the troubadours.
Bending forward, he did not look directly into the eyes of the animal,
who cocked his head, thought for a moment, and started wagging his tail.

Skills

Blondin made a fortune walking back and forth
over Niagara Falls on a tightrope—blindfolded,
or inside a sack, or pushing a wheelbarrow, or perched on stilts,
or lugging a man on his back. Once, halfway across,
he sat down to cook and eat an omelet.

Houdini, dumped into Lake Michigan chained
and locked in a weighted trunk, swam back to the boat
few moments later. He could swallow more than a hundred needles
and some thread, then pull from between his lips
the needles hanging at even intervals.

I can close my eyes and see your house
explode in a brilliant flash, silently,
with a complete absence of vibration. And when I open them again,
my heart in my mouth, everything is standing
just as before, but not as if nothing had happened.

Disappearances

Your first pocketknife, that speckled stone
the ocean smoothed, a hand-carved ivory button—
do they vanish in a blue flash that leaves
a trace of ozone? In a momentary whisper

as of silk on skin or wind in the leaves?
Weightless in the privacy of being
unobserved as they rise toward a door
in the air that sighs as it opens and closes?

Water trembles in a glass—it can hardly wait
to achieve the status of a cloud. The edges of an object
look like blurred horizons when all those molecules
start revving their tiny engines, preparing

to take off for that dimension where anything
anyone ever lost is to be found—*lost*
to us meaning *found* to the item itself.
Think about it. As you read these words,

a million needles are flying out of this world
like drops of water haloing a dog shaking herself
after a dip in the ocean. Along with teaspoons.
wedding rings, little pieces of paper with numbers on them,

half of almost any pair of socks. And not just
tables and chairs, but the contents of entire houses,
the houses themselves, cruise ships full of giddy vacationers,
small towns, the occasional city—disappearances

requiring only that the rest of us be kept forever in the dark.
So much for your iPhone, your sunglasses,
the only photo of her face how many years ago. So much
for the car keys now almost invisible on the table

in the ill-lit hallway you turn to look back down, remembering
all over again the leaf-strewn homeward path
children in stories since stories began
search for and never recover.

Tisane

[. . . from the Greek ptisane, *from* ptissein, *to crush]*

The bag puffs up in the cup
as boiling water drills from the kettle's spout
into a sudden somersaulting
of almost invisible dogs chasing their tails,
roiling the pent-up herbs into a dizzy
confusion, an infusion of blurs,
a steamy millrace. Waiting
for the right moment to suspend
the chemistry, I seem to be looking down
from a greater and greater height,
like a balloonist embarked on one of those
self-indulgent, highly publicized attempts
that always seem to end in a welter of news
reports whose only point in common is
the inhospitable desert of southern Algeria.

Van Gogh and the Wind

He heard it in the rosebushes
and flowering oleander crowding the garden of the asylum

in Saint-Rémy, in a "bread crust"–colored wheatfield extending
as far as a solitary cypress, in staked-out vines that burned in the sun.

He heard it coursing through some weather-broken pines
against a reddish late afternoon sky, shaking

the yellow leaves of lime trees in the park, fanning the green flames
of olive grove after olive grove, cedars

shading a cedar walk, a great rhododendron leaning
as if in worry toward faceless, bundled strollers. It sounded like

crickets among the cornstalks lined up at sunset behind a lone reaper,
like voices on the other side of a flowering apple orchard.

It echoed from the hills beyond a landscape with haystacks
and a rising moon, from out of the depths of a gorge called Les Peyroulets.

For a moment he heard it when he put his ear to the white blossoms
of an almond branch standing in a glass of water, and when

his eye fell on the corpse of a little brown bat, which he took back to his room
and whose wings glowed when he held the animal, with sympathy

and respect, up to the light. Once or twice he thought he heard it
in the big bunches of roses and irises he painted shortly before leaving,

"cured" at last, for the North, where he heard it again,
near Auvers, as curtains of rain swept toward him out of troubled skies,

and behind the calling of the crows that flung themselves
this way and that above the surging wheatfields

he kept returning to, nearing the day he took the pistol
with him, no knowing what he would do

until he got there, leaned his easel against a haystack,
and shot himself just below the heart. During the two days

he took to die, while shadows at his bedside loomed
and subsided and the bright sun in pictures that still came to him

fervently beat down, he listened to it. Then his brother heard him say,
I would like to go like this. And half an hour later he was gone.

The House

One day when I was a kid, it occurred to me
that being grown up was what I'd feel like
years later standing in front of what used to be
my house, watching people I didn't know
walking around behind its brightly lit windows.
I remembered this as I eased onto the narrow dirt road
and entered the woods. The pine trees looked out of focus
in the raw March rain, but the steep, eroded
driveway hadn't changed. I coaxed the car up it,
pulled over, and sat there for a minute.
No lights were on. No one appeared.
I got out, the door closing behind me
with a faraway thump, and heard the ocean.
The house and I regarded each other.
I got the impression it didn't recognize me
—or that maybe it was pretending not to.
I walked around it, kicking aside fallen branches,
a few beer cans, a tennis ball, a half-thawed
paperback whose cover was missing.
Through the kitchen window, I could vaguely
make out a cup and saucer in the sink,
a dishrag draping the faucet, the aluminum
paper towel rack screwed to the underside of a shelf
that disappeared past the pale shade
of a table lamp. Trying the door to make sure it was locked,
I tore my sleeve on an exposed nail, so I backed off,
sat down out of the rain, and opened my thermos for a dose of coffee.
The wind came and went overhead
like the breath of whoever was standing by the bed
of whoever was already sleeping. The legs of two plastic
garden chairs poked from a tangle of spindly rhododendrons.
A crow cawed. Others did, too.
I drank a little more coffee, then poured what was left onto the ground.
My knees ached, my feet felt frozen. All my senses
told me I was coming down with the flu
—but I'd be lying if I said I wasn't enjoying myself.

Destination

How many times have you surfaced from sleep not remembering
who you are, or where,
brightness and fog drawing back to show you the familiar
still under the spell of the strange?
You think you know the narrow birch- and maple-sided path
you're walking on,
and the house, whose bony clapboard flank, obscured
by hemlocks, gleams
like approaching water. Glimpsing a weathered picket fence
in tangled undergrowth,
and maybe a ladder propped against what looks like a section of roof,
you begin to recall
making your way like a partisan through winter's final attempt
at encirclement
and wonder if the muffled crunch of your footsteps
on the frozen snow
might be somebody else's. You look behind you, see no one, and discover
breathing is easy,
beside the point, forgettable. A branch creaks, a few leaves fuss in the wind,
a crow shuffles its feathers.
It occurs to you that this could be one of those dreams
in which the awareness you're
dreaming strengthens the dream instead of wiping it out.
For a moment the trees
become those in the grey-and-white prewar photograph
on a postcard from France
you stuck in a book you shelved and never managed to reach for again.
The odor of salt water
and diesel exhaust hits you suddenly, like a shot of alcohol. When you hear
cutlery on china, people
talking, the waking city's bells like an orchestra tuning up,
you realize it's perfectly
okay that the clouds floating high overhead are beyond suggesting
the passage of time.
You quicken your pace. You're nearly there. You're there.

FROM *CORRIDOR*

The Heart

I woke up to your knocking,
convinced someone was patrolling the corridor,
hammering the doors.
The heat was intense, and I wished it was raining.
Your name came to me,
and I thought about all I'd once known about you
but forgot, and once again I saw
those glossy textbook illustrations
full of bright colors, capital letters, Latin names,
those likenesses that used to take my breath away in school.
And then I began to recall more—
the Greeks thought your purpose was to cool
the quick temper of the blood,
and it took the lucid Harvey boatloads of snakes
and apes and other far-fetched creatures
to bring your secret to light.
Now I'm standing by the window,
noting the haze, the faintness of the stars,
but thinking of you, little fist
clenching and unclenching as if determined
to keep at it forever,
snug as a treasure carefully packed for shipment
to a distant museum. And I think of Byron
staring into the flames near the water's edge,
and of what he wrote afterward to Moore, ". . . all
of Shelley was consumed but for the *heart*."
Wherever you are—
in the open chest of the accusatory martyr
who leaned toward me one day in an Italian church,
or on the sleeves of the young, the madly
hopeful and in love—you do what you must,
solitary stoker down there in the body's hold,
bending to your labor,
inspired, certain of yourself. Pure and blind.

From the 1929 Edition of the Encyclopedia Britannica

for Adam Zagajewski

The Himalayas are unclimbed,
politely marveled at.

A smiling technician poses
in the jaws of an electric generator.

A hearty account, with diagrams,
of the types of decisive attack
favored by Alexander the Great.

A short entry on Lithuania
("an independent European Republic"),
the Japanese tea ceremony in twenty-seven plates,
and "a nomad fakir of India"
reading his prayers on a bed of nails.

In the Krupp works in Essen the freshly cast
steel frame of a larger riveter
hangs from the ceiling
like an industrial version of Rembrandt's
Flayed Ox.

Mussolini is "an Italian statesman" with
"obvious honesty of purpose."

A trained eagle gathers to land
on the fist of a man wearing a fencing mask,
a horsehide glove, and a double
leather sleeve for his left arm.

Sufficiency

Dozens of burning, fish-shaped clouds dove for the horizon,
determined to make more of an already explosive sunset.

The sea gave the shore another friendly pat on the back.
Crickets started singing in the dry grass beyond the wide-open door.

The day's last excursion boat glided past the window, white as a gull.
We were about to sit down around the kitchen table

and serve ourselves from a hot bowl those little red potatoes
the whole island survived on during the war.

(Bréhat)

The Children's Crusade

Next comes a little town
with a First Congregational Church
and a restaurant called The Lobster Pit.
We're thirsty after so many countries.
I drink a glass of water and try to remember
where we started from and think about
how when you forget something
it means your brain cells are dying.
A waiter brings us food in the parking lot.
I eat some fried clams and stand on my head.
I know there's such a thing as smart food—
nobody has to tell me Nature has her ways.
Today the countryside flew past our bus so fast
I couldn't count the crows on snow or the cows
lining up for their barns or the kids
playing hockey with sticks and stones
on little lakes that kept changing shape
even though each one was frozen.
But so what? Winter doesn't mean much
when it comes to the way things look at you
funny when you look at them. Any season,
it's the same old world, squiggly lines and shapes
that become tall puddles when you're close enough
to see how they shine, all fuzzy and worn-out
at the edges—houses, trees, clouds leaning toward us
with friendly expressions, wanting us to wait,
but falling behind, getting smaller and smaller,
like everybody who said, You're safer with us, don't go.
But we did, and it was like waking up
and finding my best dream staying with me
in a completely new kind of waking up,
telling me, "Well, now I'm going to be your real life."

Recalling the Huns

We knew they were coming, the people
who lived on the shores of the Frozen Ocean,
a race, according to ancient records,
savage beyond parallel. Word reached us
they'd crossed the Volga, driving the Alani
before them, whom our government then allowed to settle
in great numbers in the northern district,
where, in poverty and exhaustion, they wondered
what they were guilty of that deserved such punishment.
Refugees began arriving with starker reports.
At birth the cheeks of the Huns are scarred by an iron,
causing hairlessness, which they take as a sign of beauty.
The Huns have no need of fire or shelter and disdain
well-flavored food, preferring to feed
on herbs and tubers such as they find on the plains,
or on the half-raw flesh of any animal,
which they warm against the backs of their horses
as they journey onward. And no longer from hearsay,
but from firsthand accounts, we learned of
their fondness for surprising their enemies,
their willfulness in negotiation, their contempt
for the gods, their unbridled love of gold.
And we knew we lay directly in the path
of their advance. What could we do,
given the speed and force of their onset,
their tirelessness in pursuit? How could we expect mercy
if not one among them could tell where he was born,
having been conceived and raised as if on the waves of a torrent,
carried along in a storm over unheard-of distances?
Then came the morning I saw twelve of them
at the eastern edge of this very field.
Clearly outlined against the arrival of fair weather,
they seemed to have risen up out of the earth, small
on their stocky mounts, smaller than I could have imagined,
some carrying lances, some those terrible bows,

a little wind stirring the feathers of their helmets.
I knew they'd seen me—how could they not have?
They made no sound as they drew together to confer
and study the four directions, looking—grouped in
silhouette—like one of those many-legged, many-minded
creatures we remember from the tales of our ancestors.

The Sighting

The surface darkening maybe half a mile offshore
as if to a gust of wind, then five or six
coils rising and falling in single file,
shining, clearly *there* as she squints toward the late
afternoon sun, shading her eyes,
feeling her heart rise to the occasion, wondering
if she's actually been singled out and chosen
to see in the next instant a face rising
from the ocean's million dents, perhaps that of a dog
with bat-like ears, the face she noticed once
in a granite panorama above the portals
of a French cathedral, the saved going this way,
everyone else going that, but here
and now looking around, clearly scanning
the waters, the shoreline farther off
and the bluffs above, not failing to recognize
the human figure there whose very immobility
prompts the impulse to turn toward it and investigate—

while she keeps asking it to pause
in its actual, unresponsive progress, not sure she hears
a sound she's never heard before, hoarse clanging
like bells and static, but willing to settle for
the slightest sign from whatever it is
as it continues leftward, more and more out of her hands,
like yesterday or only a minute ago, a few recursive glints
in its wake suggesting the presence of a real
unknown creature, but one so involved
in the element of its unconcern that when she looks again
she sees nothing but a final, momentary flare
of smithereens as the sun vanishes, her sighting
already something other than what meets the eye,
restored to those shadowy canyons where green
disappears into the depths of night, the first stars
becoming distinct, and the stillness around her
no longer listening as she closes her eyes
for one more wordless attempt at calling it back.

FROM *SECOND SIGHT*

The Hydrant

Only one exists.
Its unimaginable speed
obviates the need for others.
In fact, though nothing could act
less disposed to move,
have less an air
of imminence about it, the hydrant
is the world's sole figment
of what ought to be called
the state of absolute
motion, of the principle of being
everywhere at once.
Its nature is constant,
instantaneous transit.
When you see two, three, more,
near and farther along
some eventless neighborhood prospect,
it's the hydrant
in full oscillation, seeming many
through a series of lightning
shifts from one spot
to others. When night
is torn open by a white fierceness
which the silhouettes of firefighters
look arranged against, as in
the classic tabloid
photograph, the hydrant
is always near enough to water
to sustain its appearances: that squat nubbin,
red, yellow, or black,
newly installed,
or rusted, grass-choked, on its side
in front of a tenement
slated for demolition—
that thumb with warts on it

down there on the corner nearest your house.
But who could have known
the hydrant is swiftly
and forever so alone?
Whoever took the time
to look twice and question
its regardless immobility?
We see what we want to see,
or what some system
for which there is no longer,
or not yet, a term
fitting our whereabouts, wants
us to believe. And who can tell
how many other objects we depend on
also have minds of their own,
their own methods of concealment, are also
reasons why we know things
are never as they seem?

Here Everything Is Still Floating

for Nicanor Parra

I'm walking
through the mystery
and melancholy of
a street that isn't
a piece of my world
anymore, but a slope
animated by its own
grey lilt, a slow swirl
at the edge of the sea.
Here everything is still
floating in a continuous
aftermath of flood
conditions: a little bayside
café which smells
of old cooking, the people
inside who may or may not
be waiting for more.
I sit down near a window
and order coffee expensive
enough to be thick
and sweet. A woman
at the bar starts singing,
I plan to build
a sort of pyramid there
where we can spend
the rest of our days.
I think of my Uncle
August, the unhappy
inventor, whose denials
of the never seen led to
his sudden disappearance
in a coastal fog.
Recalling the confusion

and fear I felt the day
he waved goodbye,
I look out the window
and notice a cloud
shaped like a bird,
and a surprisingly soft
night feathering near.

Giacometti's Dog

While he jogs
head down toward
the memory of a taste,
a voice, a moment
of doorway,

his front legs
constantly fail
to correct his hindquarters'
sleepy need to travel
somewhere else.

Only his narrow,
low-slung muzzle
gives the rest of him
reason to follow.

His skin
is a thin blanket
thrown over the old argument
of his skeleton
to keep the rain out
and the dry guts in.

Each step he takes
is an achievement
of what remains
ready at any moment
to become less
than the sum of its parts.

But whenever paw hits
pavement, the shock
ripples down or up his knobby

spine, his bones are shaken
into cooperation,

and all of him
settles into motion
continuous as the
twist of water
in the gutter beside him.

Ready to cross the wet street,
he glances at the traffic,
eyes glowing
zeroes, neon and fathomless
before they dim
into a green of sea-worn glass
as he looks the other way.

Guests

This morning out on the fairgrounds
they found the footprints, the same ones
I described to the Professor

the night he disappeared.
I recall his departure as clearly
as if I'd wanted it to happen.

There had been rain for a week.
He followed the winding path
from the house through the pines

down to the lake while everyone else
stayed inside playing bridge
and arguing about bird migrations.

Later I refused to answer questions.
I knew I had to think of something—
a witness, another codicil,

whatever tightened in my head
when the house started filling up
with strangers, drinking

and dancing, crazy parties.
I couldn't stand it, so I finally
locked myself in the library,

turned off the lights.
For hours I stood at the window
trying to imagine how long

it takes to travel to the great
nerve centers of the world. And
the sunset persisted, as if

waiting for the right moment
to illuminate the facts from which
I'm always about to awaken.

Memories of the Dictator

1

Sleeping with somebody, he'd use
the *bel canto* technique, which was
difficult, he said, but very beautiful.
He took care of himself—watched
what he ate, got plenty of rest.
Sometimes he took a cure.

His tastes were simple:
four or five cigarettes
over a *National Geographic*,
children's stories for
the warm feeling of the shoes
filling up with nostalgia.

Remember the old lady who left
her vital organs to her cat?
Or the disappointed heart surgeon
who ate the aneurysm?
What you've heard may be true,
and this is where he comes in.

2

Understand, he knew nothing
before he discovered that the
ballistic properties of memory
were what kept him from falling
toward his fondest target—
to become anything you needed,
wanted to afford, or thought
you should die for.

Millions loved the exoticism
of his law of personal gravity,
but finally observers began

to report that "camouflage"
wasn't the right term for explaining
the disappearance of the man
who resembled him like a brother.

3

For twenty years of bad nights
he'd dream his commands
were extended slips of the tongue.
Each morning he'd make a list
of his latest insights,
writing them down on his clothes,
stray envelopes, tables and chairs.
And finding he still couldn't read them
he'd offer huge rewards
to any hammer-brain who could manage
to break down wind-code,
star-code, cloud-code.

4

He tried to keep calm throughout
a life of periodic terrors, hoping
the first time for anything
is really the second, but in one
of his late diaries he suspects
that being a genius is like
being married to a troll
and starving to death. Pain
stopped minding its own business
in his chest. An international team
of doctors argued and published
disorderly theories. The colonels
stopped talking. His shadow trailed
a rope only he could see.

5

Few will discuss it now,
but more and more believe
in his return. They say
he will come to himself some evening
in his special graveyard, convinced
he didn't go far enough. A man in sunglasses
and a white suit will get out of a cab
at the edge of the capital and enter
a restaurant. "When was the last time
you saw him alive?" he will cry out.
"What's all this about
a fire? Who said anything
about a corpse in the ashes?"
And everyone will stop eating,
unable to remember the answers.

The Spell

The witch is dancing
for the bride and groom
in red-hot iron shoes
heavier than doorstops.
Her former servants

wager on how long she'll last,
then in rough chorus count
each step she manages until her eyes
roll up and she waves her arms
in a final, ridiculous effort to fly.

Hand in hand with her lucky
simpleton, the princess
hovers in the charmed air, nodding
and smiling on the sacrifice.
Her new dress could have been made
from the petals of those huge

white flowers which so frightened her
years ago in the forest.
They glowed like faces in the dark
and called her by her name.

Now she is
her own source of light, an intricate,
bell-shaped lamp ascending
toward a likelihood
no one looking up at her can calculate.

The guests are shouting
and knocking each other down
trying to see better. Some put on
animal masks and dance on the tables,

scattering what's left of the buffet.
In a corner six pale musicians
sit at attention with their eyes closed.

A seventh keeps clubbing his drum
to a rhythm that struggles
to come back to him.

It occurs to me I can't remember
the magic word for wakefulness, or uncle,

and a man with a fox's face
appears beside me, smelling of barnyard,
a few feathers stuck to his muzzle,
picking his teeth
with a chicken bone.

He says something in German and jabs
a paw in the direction
of the royal pair already small
and drifting in shreds of luminous blue
cloud near the topmost arches
of the hall. Suddenly every one of us

breathes in deeply
at the same moment. But whoever is
walking over our graves
takes his time:

late afternoon sunlight splays
through the cloverleaf mullions
behind me and wanders
over tapestry and stone wall
like the fingers of a blind man's hand,

while outside and seemingly far away
a dog's barking sounds like someone
hammering nails.
Then a plate hits the floor
with a solitary clang
that echoes in a widening funnel of alarm.

The spell falters, the raucous milling
breaks back on us from silence
and a faint memory of better judgement.

And as gusts of applause rise
from the crowd toward the new
inhabitants of guesswork and altitude,
the fox resumes his story in my ear,
this time, in spite of his accent.
talking my language.

Notes

New Poems

"A Few Things I Learned from Aldo Buzzi": Buzzi (1910–2009): see his *Journey to the Land of the Flies & Other Travels* (1996).

"Among the Russians": "guilty and cursed": see *The Collected Tales of Nikolai Gogol*, tr. Pevear & Volokhonsky.

"Beethoven": The Hillary Step used to be the final crux just below the summit of Mt. Everest.

"Tell Me About It": *Si rispetta il cane per il padrone*. Corsican adage = *Respect for the dog, respect for the master.*

"Baltic Rain": Mankell (1948–2015), Swedish novelist ("No person is without a shadow"); Wallander, main character in Mankell's police novels; Skøne, southernmost county in Sweden.

"The Museum": Dix (1891–1969), painter, key figure in the New Objectivity movement in 1920s Germany.

Journey to the Lost City

"Skills": Blondin—stage name of Jean-François Gravelet (1824–1897), the legendary tightrope walker and acrobat.

"Kurt Schwitters's Real Name": Schwitters (1887–1947), German expressionist / dadaist painter and collagist.

2014
Night Bus to the Afterlife, Peter Cooley
Alexandria, Jasmine Bailey
Dear Gravity, Gregory Djanikian
Pretenders, Jeff Friedman
How I Went Red, Maggie Glover
All That Might Be Done, Samuel Green
Man, Ricardo Pau-Llosa
The Wingless, Cecilia Llompart

2015
The Octopus Game, Nicky Beer
The Voices, Michael Dennis Browne
Domestic Garden, John Hoppenthaler
We Mammals in Hospitable Times, Jynne Dilling Martin
And His Orchestra, Benjamin Paloff
Know Thyself, Joyce Peseroff
cadabra, Dan Rosenberg
The Long Haul, Vern Rutsala
Bartram's Garden, Eleanor Stanford

2016
Something Sinister, Hayan Charara
The Spokes of Venus, Rebecca Morgan Frank
Adult Swim, Heather Hartley
Swastika into Lotus, Richard Katrovas
The Nomenclature of Small Things, Lynn Pedersen
Hundred-Year Wave, Rachel Richardson
Where Are We in This Story, Sarah Rosenblatt
Inside Job, John Skoyles
Suddenly It's Evening: Selected Poems, John Skoyles

2017
Disappeared, Jasmine V. Bailey
Custody of the Eyes, Kimberly Burwick
Dream of the Gone-From City, Barbara Edelman
Sometimes We're All Living in a Foreign Country, Rebecca Morgan Frank
Rowing with Wings, James Harms
Windthrow, K. A. Hays

We Were Once Here, Michael McFee
Kingdom, Joseph Millar
The Histories, Jason Whitmarsh

2018
World Without Finishing, Peter Cooley
May Is an Island, Jonathan Johnson
The End of Spectacle, Virginia Konchan
Big Windows, Lauren Moseley
Bad Harvest, Dzvinia Orlowsky
The Turning, Ricardo Pau-Llosa
Immortal Village, Kathryn Rhett
No Beautiful, Anne Marie Rooney
Last City, Brian Sneeden
Imaginal Marriage, Eleanor Stanford
Black Sea, David Yezzi

2019
The Complaints, W. S. Di Piero
Brightword, Kimberly Burwick
Ordinary Chaos, Kimberly Kruge
Blue Flame, Emily Pettit
Afterswarm, Margot Schilpp

2020
Build Me a Boat: Words for Music 1968–2018, Michael Dennis Browne
Sojourners of the In-Between, Gregory Djanikian
The Marksman, Jeff Friedman
Disturbing the Light, Samuel Green
Any God Will Do, Virginia Konchan
My Second Work, Bridget Lowe
Flourish, Dora Malech
Petition, Joyce Peseroff
Take Nothing, Deborah Pope

2021
The One Certain Thing, Peter Cooley
The Knives We Need, Nava EtShalom
Oh You Robot Saints!, Rebecca Morgan Frank

Dark Harvest: New & Selected Poems, 2001–2020, Joseph Millar
Glorious Veils of Diane, Rainie Oet
Yes and No, John Skoyles

2022
Out Beyond the Land, Kimberly Burwick
All the Hanging Wrenches, Barbara Edelman
Anthropocene Lullaby, K. A. Hays
The Woman with a Cat on Her Shoulder, Richard Katrovas
Bel Canto, Virginia Konchan
There's Something They're Not Telling Us, Kimberly Kruge
A Long Time to Be Gone, Michael McFee
Bassinet, Dan Rosenberg

2023
Night Wing over Metropolitan Area, John Hoppenthaler
Phone Ringing in a Dark House, Rolly Kent
Fleeing Actium, Ricardo Pau-Llosa
Approximate Body, Danielle Pieratti
Wild Liar, Deborah Pope
Joy Ride, Ron Slate
That Other Life, Joyce Sutphen
Sonnets with Two Torches and One Cliff, Robert Thomas

2024
Accounting for the Dark, Peter Cooley
Shine, Joseph Millar
Those Absences Now Closest, Dzvinia Orlowsky
Blue Yodel, Eleanor Stanford
Her Breath on the Window, Karenmaria Subach
Museum of the Soon to Depart, Andy Young

2025
Just About Anything, Jonathan Aaron
Goat-Footed Gods, Kathleen Driskell
Requiem, Virginia Konchan
Trying x Trying, Dora Malech
Angel Sharpening Its Beak, Michael McGriff